McGraw-Hill
Mathematics

Transition Handbook

Bridge the Gaps!

What Do I Need to Know?

Skill Builder

Challenge

2

McGraw-Hill
School Division

New York   Farmington

McGraw-Hill School Division

A Division of The McGraw·Hill Companies

Copyright © McGraw-Hill School Division,
a Division of the Educational and Professional Publishing Group of The McGraw-Hill Companies, Inc.
All rights reserved.

McGraw-Hill School Division
Two Penn Plaza
New York, New York 10121-2298

Printed in the United States of America

ISBN 0-02-100139-1 / 2

3 4 5 6 7 8 9 066 05 04 03 02 01

GRADE 2 Contents

Chapter 3
Place Value

Chapter 4
Money

Chapter 5
Add 2-Digit Numbers

Chapter 6
Subtract 2-Digit Numbers

Chapter 7
Time

Chapter 8
Data and Graphs

Chapter 9
Measurement

Chapter 10
Geometry

Chapter 11
Fractions and Probability

Chapter 12
Place Value to 1,000

Chapter 13
Add and Subtract 3-Digit Numbers

Chapter 14
Multiplication and Division

Your Handbook

Welcome to *McGraw-Hill Mathematics Transition Handbook: Bridge the Gaps!* We hope you find this handbook enjoyable as well as useful in improving your math skills.

Your teacher will assign *Skill Builder* lessons from the handbook based on the work you do on pages given to you called *What Do I Need To Know?*

Each *Skill Builder* begins with a section called *Learn,* in which a student asks *What Can I Do?* to learn a specific math skill. Stepped-out models and one or more strategies are presented that will help you strengthen that skill.

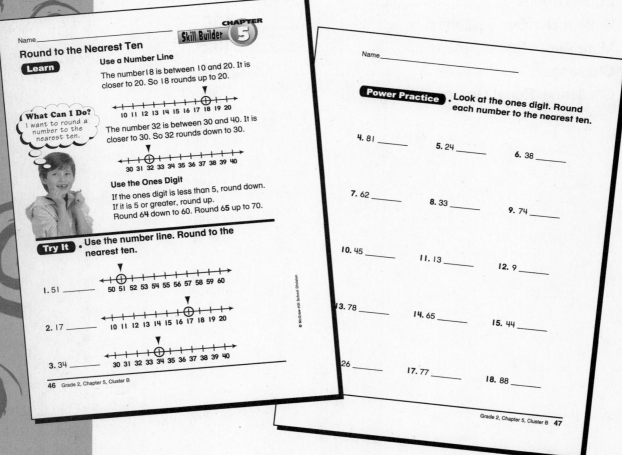

At a Glance . . .

The *Try It* section gives you a chance to try the strategy or strategies. Often the *Try It* exercises will give some hints to help you get started.

The *Power Practice* section gives you lots of opportunities to practice the lesson skill. This will help you succeed in solving the problems that come up within the corresponding chapter of your textbook.

Your teacher may assign a *Challenge* activity. Each *Challenge* provides a special math experience, such as a puzzle, code, or riddle.

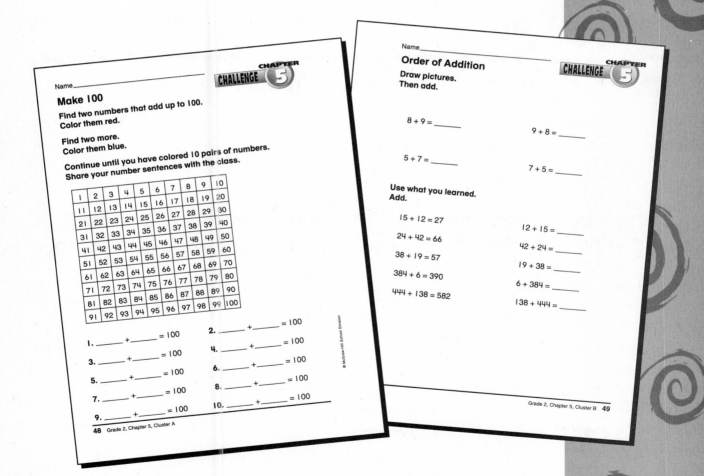

We wish you success and enjoyment in your math experiences throughout the year!

Number Line

Learn

What Can I Do?
I want to read a
number line.

Count On by Ones

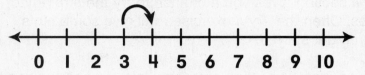

4 is 1 more than 3.

Count Back by Ones

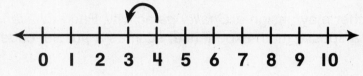

3 is 1 less than 4.

Try It • Write the missing number.

1.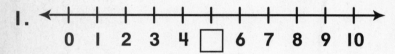

0 1 2 3 4 ☐ 6 7 8 9 10

Power Practice • Write the number that is 1 less.
Write the number that is 1 more.

	1 Less	Number	1 More
2.	4	5	6
3.	___	8	___
4.	___	2	___
5.	___	4	___

Compare Numbers

Learn

What Can I Do?
I want to compare two numbers.

Use a Number Line

These numbers go up by ones.

Numbers on the right are greater.
Numbers on the left are less.

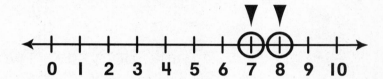

8 is greater than 7.
7 is less than 8.

Try It • Circle all the numbers greater than 5.
• Mark an X on all the numbers less than 5.

1.

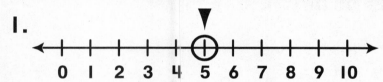

Power Practice • Use the number line.
• Circle the greater number.

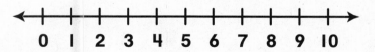

2. 4   5   **3.** 8   9   **4.** 6   5

5. 7   3   **6.** 2   6   **7.** 10   4

8. 1   3   **9.** 8   4   **10.** 0   1

Addition

Learn

What Can I Do?
I want to add across or down.

Draw a Picture

A picture can help you add. The numbers are the same across and down.

2 + 3 = ?

Think: Both say: "Two plus three."
Both have the same sum.

2 + 3 = 5

$$\begin{array}{r} 2 \\ + 3 \\ \hline \end{array}$$

$$\begin{array}{r} 2 \\ + 3 \\ \hline 5 \end{array}$$

Try It • Use the pictures.
Add across or down.

1. 2 + 1 = _____

2. $\begin{array}{r} 2 \\ + 1 \\ \hline \end{array}$

3. 3 + 4 = _____

4. $\begin{array}{r} 3 \\ + 4 \\ \hline \end{array}$

Power Practice • **Add. If you need to, draw a picture.**

5. $2 + 6 =$ _____

6. $\begin{array}{r} 2 \\ + 6 \\ \hline \end{array}$

7. $1 + 4 =$ _____

8. $\begin{array}{r} 1 \\ + 4 \\ \hline \end{array}$

9. $3 + 0 =$ _____

10. $\begin{array}{r} 3 \\ + 0 \\ \hline \end{array}$

11. $5 + 3 =$ _____

12. $\begin{array}{r} 5 \\ + 3 \\ \hline \end{array}$

Addition Facts to 8

Learn

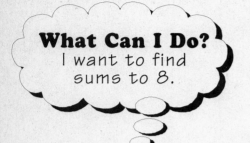

What Can I Do?
I want to find
sums to 8.

Count On

Start with the first number.
Count on to find the sum.

4 + 2 = ?

Think: 4 and 1 more is 5, and 1 more is 6.

Draw a Picture

Use a picture to help you add.

2 + 5 = ?

Draw 2 circles and 5 more circles.

Count all the circles to find the sum.

Try It • Add.

1. 3 + 1 = _____

2. 5
   + 3

3. 4 + 4 = _____

4. 2
   + 4

Name_____

Power Practice • **Add. Count on or draw a picture.**

5. $3 + 3 =$ _____

6. $1 + 5 =$ _____

7. $2 + 3 =$ _____

8. $3 + 4 =$ _____

9. $\begin{array}{r} 5 \\ + 2 \\ \hline \end{array}$

10. $\begin{array}{r} 3 \\ + 5 \\ \hline \end{array}$

11. $\begin{array}{r} 2 \\ + 6 \\ \hline \end{array}$

12. $\begin{array}{r} 6 \\ + 1 \\ \hline \end{array}$

Subtraction Facts to 8

Learn

What Can I Do?
I want to subtract from numbers up to eight.

Count Back

Start with the greater number.
Count back to find the difference.

$7 - 2 = ?$

Think: 7 and 1 less is 6, and 1 less is 5.

Draw a Picture

Use a picture to help you subtract.

$4 - 1 = ?$

Draw 4 circles. Cross out 1 circle.

Count the circles that are left to find the difference.

Try It • **Subtract.**

1. $2 - 1 =$ _____

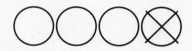

2. $\begin{array}{r} 6 \\ -3 \\ \hline \end{array}$

3. $7 - 3 =$ _____

4. $\begin{array}{r} 3 \\ -0 \\ \hline \end{array}$

Power Practice • Subtract. Count back or use a picture.

5. 8 − 2 = _____

6. 5 − 3 = _____

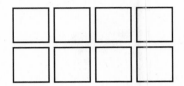

7. 2 − 2 = _____

8. 7 − 4 = _____

9. 6
     − 2

10. 3
      − 2

11. 8
      − 5

12. 4
      − 3

Addition Paths

Can you guess which path has the greatest sum?
Circle it. Then add each path to check your guess.

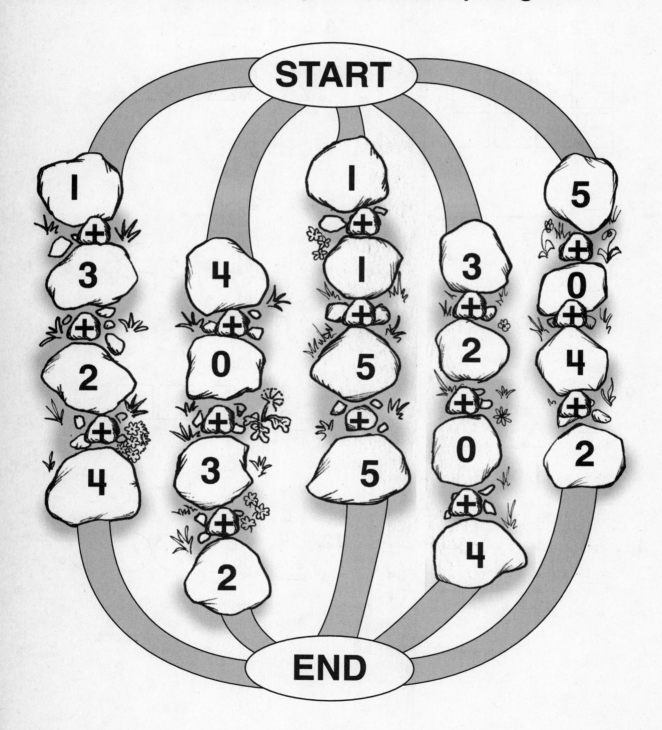

Make 5

**How many ways can you make 5?
Write each missing number and sign.**

$0 + 5 = 5$ $5 - 0 = 5$

$1\ \square\ \square = 5$ $6 - 1 = 5$

$2\ \square\ \square = 5$ $7\ \square\ \square = 5$

$3\ \square\ \square = 5$ $8\ \square\ \square = 5$

$4\ \square\ \square = 5$

$5\ \square\ \square = 5$

Add and Subtract One

Learn

What Can I Do?
I want to add and subtract one.

Use a Number Line

Count on one to add 1. Count back one to subtract 1.

Count On or Back

Count on to add.
Count back to subtract.

7 and 1 more is 8
7 and 1 less is 6

0 1 2 3 4 5 6 7 8 9 10

$7 + 1 = 8$
$7 - 1 = 6$

Try It • Use the number line. Add or subtract.

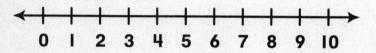

0 1 2 3 4 5 6 7 8 9 10

1. $4 + 1 =$ _____

2. $4 - 1 =$ _____

3. $2 + 1 =$ _____

4. $2 - 1 =$ _____

Power Practice • Add or subtract.

5. $6 + 1 =$ _____

6. $6 - 1 =$ _____

7. $1 + 1 =$ _____

8. $1 - 1 =$ _____

9. $8 + 1 =$ _____

10. $8 - 1 =$ _____

Name_____

Tens and Ones

Learn

What Can I Do?
I want to write a two-digit number.

Circle Ten

Find and circle ten.
Then count the ones
that are left.

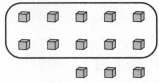

1 ten   3 ones
The number is 13.

Count Ones

Count ones.
Then write the number
using tens and ones.

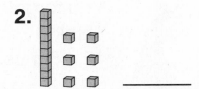

1   2   3   4   5

6   7   8   9   10

11   12   13   14   15

The number is 15.

Try It • Write each number.

1. _____

2. _____

Power Practice • Circle ten. Write each number.

3. _____

4. _____

5. _____

6. _____

Addition and Subtraction Facts to 12

Learn

Draw a Picture

A picture can help you add or subtract.

$4 + 6 = ?$

What Can I Do?
I forgot an addition or subtraction fact!

The plus sign means add. $4 + 6 = 10$

$$\begin{array}{r} 11 \\ -\ 3 \\ \hline 8 \end{array}$$

The minus sign means subtract. $11 - 3 = 8$

Use Facts You Know

You forgot $12 - 5$. You know $10 - 5 = 5$.
Think: 12 is 2 more than 10.
$12 - 5$ must be 2 more than $10 - 5$.
So, $12 - 5 = 7$.

Try It • Watch the signs. Add or subtract.

1. $2 + 9 = $ _____

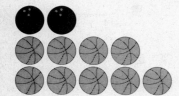

2. $\begin{array}{r} 12 \\ -\ 8 \\ \hline \end{array}$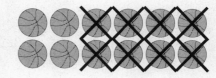

3. $9 - 7 = $ _____

4. $\begin{array}{r} 3 \\ +\ 7 \\ \hline \end{array}$

Name_____

Power Practice • Add or subtract. Draw a picture or use facts you know.

5. 2 + 7 = _____

6. 5
       + 6

7. 11 − 4 = _____

8. 8
       + 4

9. 10 − 9 = _____

10. 9
        − 4

11. 5 + 7 = _____

12. 11
        − 6

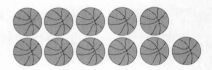

Write a Number Sentence

Learn

What Can I Do?
I want to write a number sentence to match a picture.

Choose the Operation

Look at the picture. Decide whether to add or subtract. Choose + or −.

Think: A group of 4 is joining a group of 6. I can add to find how many in all.

$$4 + 6 = 10$$

Use the Picture

Count to find how many in all. Count to find how many are taken away.

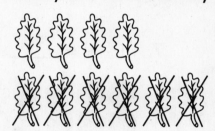

Think: There are 10 in all. 6 are crossed out. I can subtract to find how many are left.

$$10 - 6 = 4$$

Try It • Write a number sentence to match each picture.

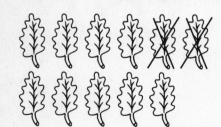

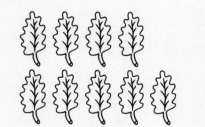

1. _____ ◯ _____ ◯ _____   2. _____ ◯ _____ ◯ _____

Name_____

Power Practice . Write a number sentence to match each picture.

3. ___ ◯ ___ ◯ ___

4. ___ ◯ ___ ◯ ___

5. ___ ◯ ___ ◯ ___

6. ___ ◯ ___ ◯ ___

Sum Puzzles

**In each puzzle, follow the arrows.
The sum of the numbers across or
down is the number in the center.**

2	6	
5	12	4
	3	4

	1	5
6	14	2
0	7	

9	0	
2	16	1
	3	8

Make Up Number Sentences

Look at the picture.

What can you add?
What can you subtract?

Write four number sentences.
Ask a friend to solve them.

1. ___ ◯ ___ ◯ ___

2. ___ ◯ ___ ◯ ___

3. ___ ◯ ___ ◯ ___

4. ___ ◯ ___ ◯ ___

Hundred Chart

Learn

What Can I Do?
I don't remember some numbers to 100.

Find Patterns in a Hundred Chart

Here are the first three rows of a hundred chart.

1	2	3	4	5	6	7	8	9	10
11	12	13	14	15	16	17	18	19	20
21	22	23	24	25	26	27	28	29	30

A hundred chart shows the order of numbers.
It shows number patterns, too.
How can the chart help you count by 10s?
How can it help you count by 5s?
How can you tell which numbers are greater?
How can you tell which numbers are less?

Try It • **Fill in the missing numbers.**

1.

1	2	3	4	5	6	7	8	9	10
11	12	13	14	15	16	17	18	19	
21	22	23	24	25	26	27	28	29	
31	32	33	34	35	36	37	38	39	
41	42	43	44	45	46	47	48	49	
51	52	53	54	55	56	57	58	59	
61	62	63	64	65	66	67	68	69	70
71	72	73	74	75	76	77	78	79	80
81	82	83	84	85	86	87	88	89	90
91	92	93	94	95	96	97	98	99	100

Power Practice • Fill in the missing numbers.

2.

1	2	3	4	5	6	7	8	9	10
11	12	13	14		16	17	18	19	20
21	22	23	24		26	27	28	29	30
31	32	33	34		36	37	38	39	40
41	42	43	44		46	47	48	49	50
51	52	53	54		56	57	58	59	60
61	62	63	64		66	67	68	69	70
71	72	73	74		76	77	78	79	80
81	82	83	84		86	87	88	89	90
91	92	93	94		96	97	98	99	100

3.

1	2	3	4		6	7	8	9	
11	12	13	14		16	17	18	19	
21	22	23	24		26	27	28	29	
31	32	33	34		36	37	38	39	
41	42	43	44		46	47	48	49	
51	52	53	54	55	56	57	58	59	60
61	62	63	64	65	66	67	68	69	70
71	72	73	74	75	76	77	78	79	80
81	82	83	84	85	86	87	88	89	90
91	92	93	94	95	96	97	98	99	100

Place-Value Chart

Learn

Use a Place-Value Chart

This place-value chart shows tens and ones.
Tens are on the left.
Ones are on the right.

tens	ones
3	4

There are 3 tens and 4 ones in 34.

Rename Ones as Tens and Ones

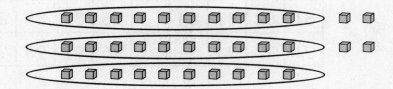

This shows 3 tens with 4 left over.

tens	ones
3	4

What Can I Do?
I want to write a number as tens and ones.

Try It • Write each number in a place-value chart.

1. 59

tens	ones

2. 17

tens	ones

3. 40

tens	ones

4. 62

tens	ones

Power Practice • Write each number.

5. _____
tens	ones
5	2

6. _____
tens	ones
3	7

7. _____
tens	ones
I	I

8. _____
tens	ones
7	5

9. _____
tens	ones
4	8

10. _____
tens	ones
6	6

11. _____
tens	ones
9	0

12. _____
tens	ones
I	4

13. _____
tens	ones
2	3

14. _____
tens	ones
8	2

15. _____
tens	ones
0	9

16. _____
tens	ones
4	5

Identify Reasonable Estimates

Learn

Use Number Sense

Do you think there are more or fewer than 50 fish? Do you think there are more or fewer than 10 fish?

It looks like there are more than 10 and fewer than 50. A good estimate is 20 or 30 fish.

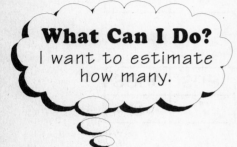

What Can I Do?
I want to estimate how many.

Group Tens to Estimate

You can estimate how many by grouping tens. There are nearly 3 tens, or 30 fish.

Try It • Circle the best estimate.

1. 2   20   200

Power Practice • Circle the best estimate.

2. 10   30   100

3. 10   30   50

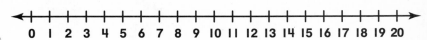
Greater Than and Less Than

Learn

Use a Number Line

Numbers on the right are greater.
Numbers on the left are less.

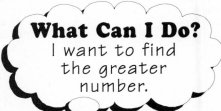

What Can I Do?
I want to find the greater number.

```
←—+—+—+—+—+—+—+—+—+—+—+—+—+—+—+—+—+—+—+—+—+—→
  0  1  2  3  4  5  6  7  8  9  10 11 12 13 14 15 16 17 18 19 20
```

Think: 14 is to the left of 16.
So, 16 is greater than 14.

Compare Place Values

Look at the tens place. Which digit is greater?
If both are the same look at the ones place.
Which digit is greater?
6 is greater than 4.
So, 16 is greater than 14.

tens	ones
1	4
1	6

Try It • **Use the number line.**
Circle the greater number.

```
←—+—+—+—+—+—+—+—+—+—+—+—+—+—+—+—+—+—+—+—+—+—→
  0  1  2  3  4  5  6  7  8  9  10 11 12 13 14 15 16 17 18 19 20
```

1. 12   2   **2.** 15   17

Power Practice • **Circle the number that is greater.**

3. 71   17   **4.** 12   21   **5.** 33   22

6. 68   67   **7.** 50   51   **8.** 39   40

Name _____

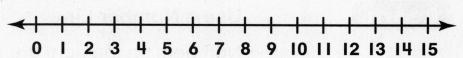

Before, After, Between

 Learn

0 1 2 3 4 5 6 7 8 9 10 11 12 13 14 15

What Can I Do?
I want to find the number between two numbers.

Use a Number Line

Think:
12 is just before 13.
12 is just after 11.
12 is between 11 and 13.

The numbers go in order from least to greatest.

11, 12, 13

Try It • Use the number line. Write the number.

0 1 2 3 4 5 6 7 8 9 10 11 12 13 14 15

1. just after 6 ____

2. just before 10 ____

3. between 15 and 17 ____

Power Practice • Write the number.

4. just after 14 ____

5. just before 18 ____

6. just after 34 ____

7. just before 59 ____

8. between 76 and 78 ____

Skip Counting by 2s

Learn

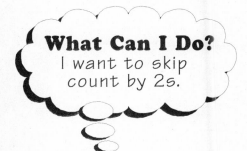

What Can I Do?
I want to skip count by 2s.

Use a Hundred Chart

Here are the first 4 rows of a hundred chart. Start with 2 and count every other number.

1	②	3	④	5	⑥	7	⑧	9	⑩
11	⑫	13	⑭	15	⑯	17	⑱	19	⑳
21	㉒	23	㉔	25	㉖	27	㉘	29	㉚
31	㉜	33	㉞	35	㊱	37	㊳	39	㊵

Use Number Patterns

Look at the ones digits.

2 4 6 8 10 12 14 16 18 20

Use the pattern "2, 4, 6, 8, 0" to decide what comes next.

Try It • **Fill in the missing numbers.**

1.

1	2	3	4	5	6	7	8	9	10
11	12	13	14	15	16	17	18	19	
21		23		25		27		29	
31		33		35		37		39	
41		43		45		47		49	50

Power Practice • **Write each missing number.**

2. 2, 4, ___, 8, 10, ___

3. 32, ___, 36, 38, 40, ___

4. 80, 82, ___, ___, 88, 90

5. 66, 68, ___, 72, ___, 76

What's the Difference?

**Find the numbers shown in the place-value charts.
Then subtract. What do you find?**

tens	ones
9	8

−

tens	ones
8	9

= _____

tens	ones
8	7

−

tens	ones
7	8

= _____

tens	ones
7	6

−

tens	ones
6	7

= _____

tens	ones
6	5

−

tens	ones
5	6

= _____

tens	ones
5	4

−

tens	ones
4	5

= _____

tens	ones
4	3

−

tens	ones
3	4

= _____

tens	ones
3	2

−

tens	ones
2	3

= _____

tens	ones
2	1

−

tens	ones
1	2

= _____

© McGraw-Hill School Division

Counting in Portuguese

**The numbers in the box are Portuguese.
They are not in order.**

**Read the clues.
Put the numbers in order.**

Write them on a number line.

| catorze |
| doze |
| onze |
| quinze |
| treze |

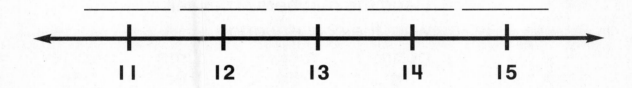

Clues

1. Doze comes just before treze.

2. Catorze comes between treze and quinze.

3. Treze is greater than onze.

Identifying Coins

Learn

What Can I Do?
I want to know how much a coin is worth.

Memorize Coin Sizes and Colors

A penny is brown.
Nickels, dimes, and quarters are silver.

A dime is small. A quarter is big.
A nickel is bigger than a dime but smaller than a quarter.

Learn What Coins Are Worth

Read the numbers. They tell what the coin is worth.

penny	nickel	dime	quarter
1¢	5¢	10¢	25¢

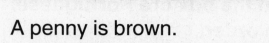

Try It • Match each coin to its name and amount.
Draw lines to match.

25¢

5¢

I. nickel

2. quarter

Power Practice • Circle the correct coin.

3. 1¢

4. 10¢

5. 5¢

Skip Count by 5s and 10s

Learn

What Can I Do?
I want to skip count by 5s and 10s.

Use Number Patterns

Look at the ones digits.

5 10 15 20 25 30

10 20 30 40 50 60

Use the pattern to decide what number comes next.

Try It • **Fill in the missing numbers.**

1.

1	2	3	4	5	6	7	8	9	
11	12	13	14		16	17	18	19	
21	22	23	24		26	27	28	29	
31	32	33	34		36	37	38	39	40

Power Practice • **Write each missing number.**

2. 25, 30, _____, 40, 45, _____

3. 40, _____, 60, 70, 80, _____

4. 50, 55, _____, _____, 70, 75

5. 20, 30, _____, 50, _____, 70

Equal Amounts

 Learn

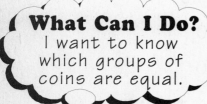

What Can I Do?
I want to know which groups of coins are equal.

Compare Coins

A quarter is worth 2 dimes and 1 nickel.
A dime is worth 2 nickels.
A nickel is worth 5 pennies.

 > > >

Skip Count to Find How Much in All

Start with one coin.
Skip count to find how much in all.

10¢, 20¢, 30¢

5¢,   10¢,   15¢

 **Try It** • Skip count to find how much in all.
In each row, circle the two groups that show the same amount.

1.

   1¢, _____   5¢, _____   _____

2.

   5¢, 10¢, _____, _____   1¢, _____   _____, _____

Name_____

3.      

4.    

5.    

6.   

Counting On

Learn

What Can I Do?
I want to count on to find how many in all.

Use a Number Line

Each number goes up by one.
Move up one to count on one.

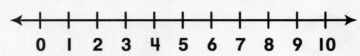

0 1 2 3 4 5 6 7 8 9 10

4 and one more is 5 and one more is 6.

Draw a Picture

Draw the number you have.
Draw 1 more. Count.
Draw 1 more. Count.

Try It • Use the number line.
Find 1 more.

0 1 2 3 4 5 6 7 8 9 10

1. 3 and 1 more = _____

2. 6 and 1 more = _____

3. 1 and 1 more = _____

4. 8 and 1 more = _____

Power Practice • Write each missing number.

5. Start with 5. 1 more makes _____. 1 more makes _____.

6. Start with 3. 1 more makes _____. 1 more makes _____.

7. Start with 7. 1 more makes _____.

1 more makes _____. 1 more makes _____.

Writing Money Two Ways

Learn

What Can I Do?
I want to write money amounts with dollar signs or cents signs.

Read $ and ¢ Symbols

The symbol ¢ is read "cents." Read 32¢ as "thirty-two cents."

The symbol $ means "dollars." Read $1.32 as "one dollar and thirty-two cents." Numbers before the decimal point are dollars. Numbers after the decimal point are cents.

Look at Place Value

A decimal point separates dollars from cents.

dollars	dimes	pennies
$1 .	3	2

Try It • **Do the numbers show the same amount? Circle yes or no.**

1. $0.60   60¢   yes   no   2. $2.50   25¢   yes   no

3. $0.43   34¢   yes   no   4. $0.95   95¢   yes   no

Power Practice • **Circle the two that show the same amount.**

5. $1.24   24¢ $0.24   6. 68¢ $0.68 $6.80

7. 53¢ $5.53 $0.53   8. $0.35   35¢ $3.05

9. $1.66   66¢ $0.66   10. $99.00 $0.99   99¢

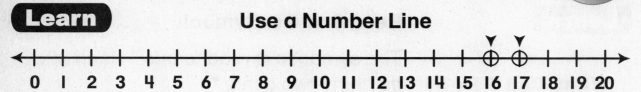

Compare Whole Numbers

Learn

Use a Number Line

0 1 2 3 4 5 6 7 8 9 10 11 12 13 14 15 16 17 18 19 20

Each number goes up by ones.
The number on the right is greater.
The number on the left is less.

17 is greater than 16. 16 is less than 17.

Look at Place Value

tens	ones
1	6
1	7

Look at the tens digits. Compare. Which digit is greater?

If the tens digits are the same, look at the ones digits. Compare. Which digit is greater?

Think: 7 ones is greater than 6 ones.
17 is greater than 16.

What Can I Do?
I want to compare two numbers.

Try It • Use the place-value charts.
Circle the number that is greater.

1.

tens	ones
3	5
3	9

2.

tens	ones
2	1
1	2

3.

tens	ones
8	3
7	3

4.

tens	ones
6	7
6	8

Name_____

Power Practice • Circle the number that is greater.

5. 68 86

6. 24 23

7. 19 91

8. 39 40

9. 27 25

10. 61 60

11. 13 11

12. 55 45

13. 98 89

14. 67 77

15. 56 50

16. 75 57

17. 22 33

18. 90 9

19. 86 68

20. 49 48

Two Ways to Pay

**The coins show one way to pay.
Think of another way.
Write the missing numbers.**

Another way to pay: _____ nickels, 4 pennies

Another way to pay: _____ nickels, 3 pennies

Another way to pay: _____ quarter, _____ nickel, _____ pennies

Another way to pay: _____ dimes, _____ nickel

Another way to pay: _____ nickels

Another way to pay: 3 dimes, _____ nickels

A Maze of Money

Make the coins add up to the amount at the bottom.
Pick one from the top row, one from the middle row,
and one from the bottom row.
Use each coin or group of coins only once.
Draw lines. The first one is done for you.

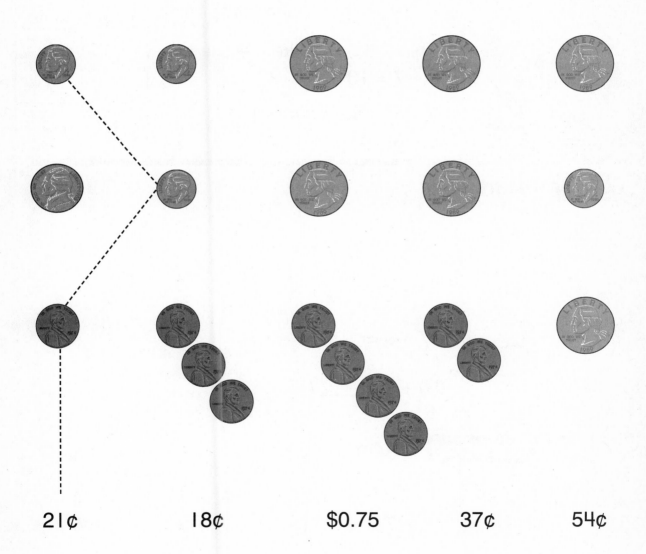

21¢   18¢ $0.75   37¢   54¢

Addition Facts to 20

Learn

What Can I Do?
I want to add
facts to 20.

Use Doubles

Think about doubles.

2 + 2 = 4	6 + 6 = 12
3 + 3 = 6	7 + 7 = 14
4 + 4 = 8	8 + 8 = 16
5 + 5 = 10	9 + 9 = 18

Think: 6 + 7 is like 6 + 6 + 1.

6 + 7 = 13

6 + 5 is like 6 + 6 − 1.

6 + 5 = 11

Use a Place-Value Chart

Keep tens and ones apart.
Use a place-value chart.

	tens	ones
		6
+		7
	1	3

Try It • Add.

1. 5 + 5 = _____   5 + 6 = _____

2. 8 + 8 = _____   8 + 7 = _____

3. 7 + 7 = _____   7 + 6 = _____

4. 9 + 9 = _____   10 + 9 = _____

Power Practice • Add.

5.	2	6.	3	7.	9	8.	7	9.	6	10.	8
	+ 8		+ 9		+ 7		+ 5		+ 9		+ 6

CHAPTER 5

Name_____

Place Value

Learn

What Can I Do?
I want to know the number of tens and ones in a number.

Use a Place-Value Chart

Write the number 34 in a place-value chart.

tens	ones
3	4

34 has 3 tens and 4 ones.

Understanding Place Value

The ones digit is on the right. The tens digit is to the left of the ones digit.

The 4 tells how many ones are in 34. The 3 tells how many tens are in 34.

Try It • Write each number in a place-value chart.

1. 78

tens	ones

2. 39

tens	ones

3. 14

tens	ones

4. 60

tens	ones

Power Practice • Write the number of tens and ones.

5. 82 _____ tens _____ ones

6. 47 _____ tens _____ ones

7. 24 _____ tens _____ ones

8. 90 _____ tens _____ ones

9. 55 _____ tens _____ ones

10. 18 _____ ten _____ ones

Regrouping Ones

Learn

Use a Place-Value Chart

Count ones.

Write the number in a place-value chart.

Tens are on the left.
Ones are on the right.
There are 1 ten and 5 ones in 15.

tens	ones
1	5

What Can I Do?
I need to regroup the ones as tens and ones.

Circle Tens

Draw the number of ones.

Circle tens. Count the ones left over.

This shows 2 tens with 3 ones left over.

Try It • **Count. Circle tens.**
Write each number in a chart.

1. _____ ten _____ ones   2. _____ tens _____ ones

Power Practice • Write each number two ways.

3. _____ ones
   _____ ten _____ ones

4. _____ ones
   _____ tens _____ ones

5. _____ ones
   _____ tens _____ ones

6. _____ ones
   _____ tens _____ ones

7. _____ ones
   _____ tens _____ one

8. _____ ones
   _____ ten _____ ones

9. _____ ones
   _____ ten _____ ones

10. _____ ones
    _____ tens _____ ones

Turnaround Facts

Learn

What Can I Do?
I often forget that numbers may be added in any order.

Draw a Picture

Draw 4 dots and 6 dots. Flip the picture in any order.

Think: The numbers are the same, so the sums must be the same.

$4 + 6 = 6 + 4$

Use Facts You Know

If you know that $5 + 7 = 12$, then you know that $7 + 5 = 12$.

If you know that $4 + 3 = 7$, then you know that $3 + 4 = 7$.

Try It • **Draw a picture. Then add.**

1. $6 + 8 =$ _____ $8 + 6 =$ _____

2. $7 + 4 =$ _____ $4 + 7 =$ _____

Name_____

Power Practice • Add.

3. $5 + 8 =$ _____

$8 + 5 =$ _____

4. $7 + 6 =$ _____

$6 + 7 =$ _____

5. $9 + 7 =$ _____

$7 + 9 =$ _____

6. $4 + 9 =$ _____

$9 + 4 =$ _____

7. $3 + 6 =$ _____

$6 + 3 =$ _____

8. $8 + 4 =$ _____

$4 + 8 =$ _____

9. $3 + 9 =$ _____

$9 + 3 =$ _____

10. $7 + 8 =$ _____

$8 + 7 =$ _____

Round to the Nearest Ten

Learn

Use a Number Line

The number 18 is between 10 and 20. It is closer to 20. So 18 rounds up to 20.

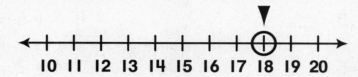

What Can I Do?
I want to round a number to the nearest ten.

The number 32 is between 30 and 40. It is closer to 30. So 32 rounds down to 30.

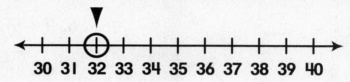

Use the Ones Digit

If the ones digit is less than 5, round down. If it is 5 or greater, round up.
Round 64 down to 60. Round 65 up to 70.

Try It • Use the number line. Round to the nearest ten.

1. 51 _____

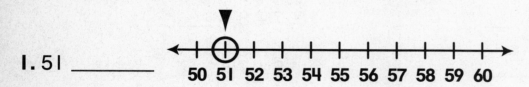

2. 17 _____

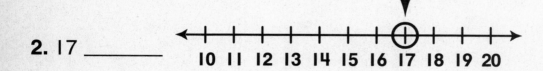

3. 34 _____

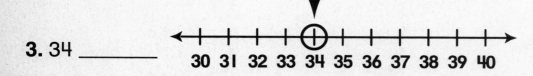

Power Practice · **Look at the ones digit. Round each number to the nearest ten.**

4. 81 _____   **5.** 24 _____   **6.** 38 _____

7. 62 _____   **8.** 33 _____   **9.** 74 _____

10. 45 _____   **11.** 13 _____   **12.** 9 _____

13. 78 _____   **14.** 65 _____   **15.** 44 _____

16. 26 _____   **17.** 77 _____   **18.** 88 _____

Make 100

Find two numbers that add up to 100.
Color them red.

Find two more.
Color them blue.

Continue until you have colored 10 pairs of numbers.
Share your number sentences with the class.

1	2	3	4	5	6	7	8	9	10
11	12	13	14	15	16	17	18	19	20
21	22	23	24	25	26	27	28	29	30
31	32	33	34	35	36	37	38	39	40
41	42	43	44	45	46	47	48	49	50
51	52	53	54	55	56	57	58	59	60
61	62	63	64	65	66	67	68	69	70
71	72	73	74	75	76	77	78	79	80
81	82	83	84	85	86	87	88	89	90
91	92	93	94	95	96	97	98	99	100

1. _____ + _____ = 100   2. _____ + _____ = 100

3. _____ + _____ = 100   4. _____ + _____ = 100

5. _____ + _____ = 100   6. _____ + _____ = 100

7. _____ + _____ = 100   8. _____ + _____ = 100

9. _____ + _____ = 100   10. _____ + _____ = 100

Order of Addition

Draw pictures.
Then add.

$8 + 9 =$ _____

$9 + 8 =$ _____

$5 + 7 =$ _____

$7 + 5 =$ _____

Use what you learned.
Add.

$15 + 12 = 27$

$12 + 15 =$ _____

$24 + 42 = 66$

$42 + 24 =$ _____

$38 + 19 = 57$

$19 + 38 =$ _____

$384 + 6 = 390$

$6 + 384 =$ _____

$444 + 138 = 582$

$138 + 444 =$ _____

Subtraction Facts to 20

Learn

What Can I Do?
I want to subtract facts to 20.

Use Doubles

Think about doubles:
$5 + 5 = 10$ and $10 - 5 = 5$.

You can use doubles to find $11 - 6$.

Think: 11 is 1 more than 10.
$11 - 5$ is 1 more than $10 - 5$.
So, $11 - 5 = 6$.

Use a Place-Value Chart

A place-value chart helps you keep the tens and ones apart.

	tens	ones
	1	5
−		7
		8

Try It • Subtract.

1. $16 - 8 =$ _____

$17 - 8 =$ _____

2. $14 - 7 =$ _____

$15 - 7 =$ _____

3. $8 - 4 =$ _____

$9 - 4 =$ _____

4. $12 - 6 =$ _____

$13 - 6 =$ _____

Power Practice • Subtract.

5. 12
  − 8

6. 13
  − 9

7. 16
  − 7

8. 13
  − 5

9. 14
  − 8

10. 17
  − 9

Place Value

Learn

What Can I Do?
I want to know the number of tens and ones in a number.

Use a Place-Value Chart

Write the number 78 in a chart.

tens	ones
7	8

78 has 7 tens and 8 ones.

Use Expanded Notation

78 = 70 + 8
70 = 7 tens
 8 = 8 ones

78 = 7 tens 8 ones

Try It • Write each number in a place-value chart.

1. 45

tens	ones

2. 37

tens	ones

3. 23

tens	ones

4. 50

tens	ones

Power Practice • Write the number of tens and ones.

5. 61 _____ tens _____ one

6. 19 _____ ten _____ ones

7. 88 _____ tens _____ ones

8. 70 _____ tens _____ ones

9. 94 _____ tens _____ ones

10. 12 _____ ten _____ ones

Regrouping Tens and Ones

Learn

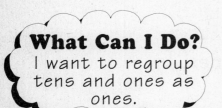

What Can I Do?
I want to regroup tens and ones as ones.

Use a Place-Value Chart and Pictures

tens	ones
1	3

There are 1 ten and 3 ones in 13.

That is the same as 13 ones. Prove it by drawing a picture.

Think About Money

1 dime = 10 pennies

You can trade 1 dime for 10 pennies.

How many pennies would you get for 2 dimes? 3 dimes? 4 dimes?

Try It • Read the place-value chart. Write the number as ones.

tens	ones
1	5

1. _____ ones

tens	ones
2	6

2. _____ ones

Power Practice • Write each number two ways.

 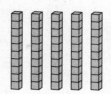

3. ____ ten ____ ones

____ ones

4. ____ tens ____ ones

____ ones

5. ____ tens ____ one

____ ones

6. ____ tens ____ ones

____ ones

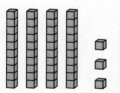

7. ____ tens ____ ones

____ ones

8. ____ tens ____ ones

____ ones

Fact Families

Learn

What Can I Do?
I can't remember all four facts in a fact family.

Write Number Sentences

Begin with an addition fact, such as 7 + 8 = 15. Put the numbers together in different addition and subtraction sentences.

7 + 8 = 15	8 + 7 = 15
15 − 8 = 7	15 − 7 = 8

The 2 addition sentences and 2 subtraction sentences make a fact family.

Use Facts You Know

If you know that 7 + 8 = 15, then you know that 8 + 7 = 15. Numbers may be added in any order.

Try It • Complete each fact family.

1. 6 + 8 = _____

   8 + 6 = _____

   14 − 8 = _____

   14 − 6 = _____

2. 7 + 3 = _____

   3 + 7 = _____

   10 − 3 = _____

   10 − 7 = _____

Power Practice • Use the numbers. Write the fact family.

3. 5, 7, 12

   _____

   _____

   _____

   _____

4. 7, 9, 16

   _____

   _____

   _____

   _____

Round to the Nearest Ten

Learn

What Can I Do?
I want to round a number to the nearest ten.

Use a Number Line

10 11 12 13 14 15 16 17 18 19 20

12 is between 10 and 20. It is closer to 10. So, 12 rounds down to 10.

17 is between 10 and 20. It is closer to 20. So 17 rounds up to 20.

Use the Ones Digit

If the ones digit is less than 5, round down. Round 14 down to 10.

If the ones digit is 5 or greater, round up. Round 15 up to 20.

Try It • Use the number line.
Round to the nearest ten.

1. 31 _____

30 31 32 33 34 35 36 37 38 39 40

2. 58 _____

50 51 52 53 54 55 56 57 58 59 60

Power Practice • Look at the ones digit. Round each number to the nearest ten.

3. 73 _____   **4.** 19 _____   **5.** 25 _____

6. 54 _____   **7.** 36 _____   **8.** 88 _____

9. 42 _____   **10.** 65 _____   **11.** 7 _____

A Difference of 15

Color only the subtraction sentences with a difference of 15.

What do you see?

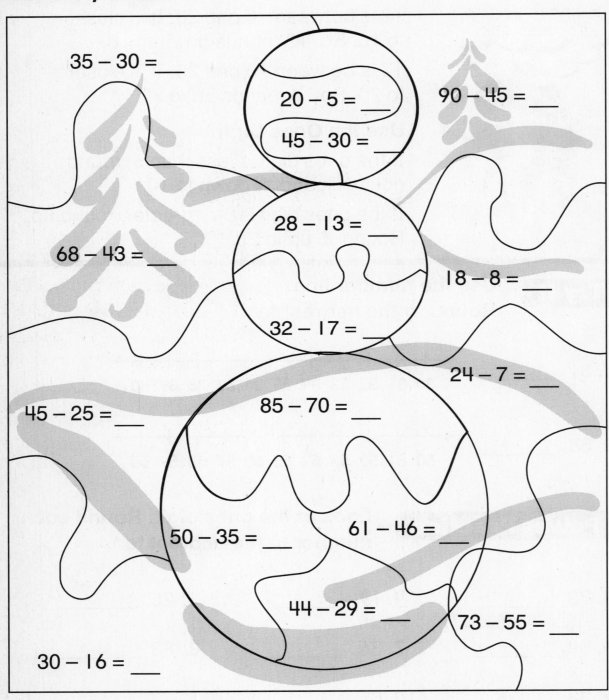

$35 - 30 =$ ___

$20 - 5 =$ ___

$45 - 30 =$ ___

$90 - 45 =$ ___

$68 - 43 =$ ___

$28 - 13 =$ ___

$18 - 8 =$ ___

$32 - 17 =$ ___

$24 - 7 =$ ___

$45 - 25 =$ ___

$85 - 70 =$ ___

$50 - 35 =$ ___

$61 - 46 =$ ___

$44 - 29 =$ ___

$73 - 55 =$ ___

$30 - 16 =$ ___

Math of Planet X

Fact families on Planet X are the same as on Earth. Numbers are different.

Here are some facts from Planet X. Complete each fact family.

◆ + ■ = ✖

_____

_____

_____

★ − ➤ = ♥

_____

_____

_____

▼ − ✔ = ■

_____

_____

_____

▲ + ♥ = ◆

_____

_____

_____

● + ▲ = ■

_____

_____

_____

Name_____

Time to the Hour

Learn

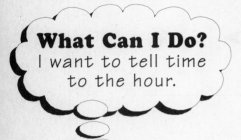

What Can I Do?
I want to tell time to the hour.

Look at the Clock Hands

The big hand shows the minutes.
The small hand shows the hours.
The minute hand points to 12
at the start of each hour. As the minute
hand moves around the clock, the hour
hand moves to the next number.

3:00   4:00

Read Times Two Ways

8 o'clock
8:00

Try It • **Write the time two ways.**

1.

_____ o'clock

_____ : _____

2.

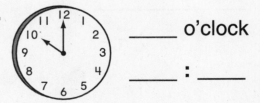

_____ o'clock

_____ : _____

Power Practice • **Write the time.**

3.

_____

_____

4.

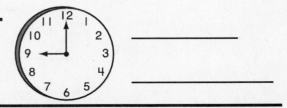

_____

_____

Time to the Half Hour

Learn

Divide the Clock in Half

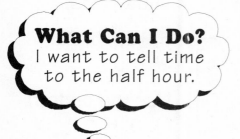

What Can I Do?
I want to tell time to the half hour.

The minute hand points to 12 at the start of each hour.
It points to 6 at the half-hour.
At the half-hour, the hour hand is between two numbers.

 3:00   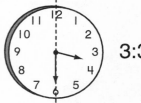 3:30

Read Times Two Ways

 half past 8
8:30

Try It • Write the time two ways.

1.    half past _____

_____ : _____

2.    half past _____

_____ : _____

Power Practice • Write the time.

3.

_____

4.

_____

5.

_____

6.

_____

Skip Count by 5s

Learn

What Can I Do?
I want to skip count by 5s.

Use a Hundred Chart

The chart shows the numbers from 1 to 100. Look at the pattern for 5s.

1	2	3	4	5	6	7	8	9	10
11	12	13	14	15	16	17	18	19	20
21	22	23	24	25	26	27	28	29	30
31	32	33	34	35	36	37	38	39	40
41	42	43	44	45	46	47	48	49	50
51	22	53	54	55	56	57	58	59	60
61	62	63	64	65	66	67	68	69	70
71	72	73	74	75	76	77	78	79	80
81	82	83	84	85	86	87	88	89	90
91	92	93	94	95	96	97	98	99	100

Use Number Patterns

Look at the ones digits.

5, 10, 15, 20, 25, 30

Use the pattern "5, 0, 5, 0, 5, 0" to decide what number comes next.

Try It • **Fill in the missing numbers.**

1.

21	22	23	24		26	27	28	29	
31	32	33	34		36	37	38	39	40
41	42	43	44		46	47	48	49	

Power Practice • **Write each missing number.**

2. 15, 20, _____, 30, 35, _____

3. 30, _____, 40, 45, 50, _____

4. 10, 15, _____, _____, 30, 35

Ordinal Numbers

Learn

Use Numbers to Count and to Order

Use the top numbers to count things. Use the bottom numbers to put things in order.

What Can I Do?
I want to use numbers to put things in order.

one	two	three	four	five	six	seven	eight	nine	ten
first	second	third	fourth	fifth	sixth	seventh	eighth	ninth	tenth

Count from 1 to 10. Put things in order from first to tenth.

Try It • Draw lines to match.

1. two -------

2. five

3. seven

fifth   seventh ------- second

Power Practice • Follow the directions.

4. Color the third duckling yellow.

5. Color the tenth duckling orange.

6. Color the sixth duckling red.

7. Color the first duckling brown.

Fun Times

Read the story.
Draw hands on the clocks to show each time in order.

It's summer vacation! Jason and his sister, Katy, wake up at 6:30 in the morning. By 7:15 they are outside in the big field. They pick berries for breakfast and return to the house by 8:00. Dad makes berry pancakes.

By 11:15 or so, the pond is warm enough for swimming. Mom and Dad take the children for rides in the rowboat. Lunch is at 12:45 on the back deck. After that, everyone reads or naps. Around 2:30, it's time for a hike in the woods. Jason calls the dogs, and the family heads out for a nice walk.

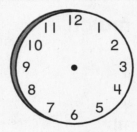

Calendar Clues

Mr. Lee's class has student helpers. Mr. Lee writes the helpers' names on the calendar.

Here is the calendar page for March. Columns run up and down. Rows run across.

Read the clues. Find out who is the helper.

MARCH

Sunday	Monday	Tuesday	Wednesday	Thursday	Friday	Saturday
			1	2 Tina	3	4
5	6 Lucia	7	8 Karif	9	10	11
12	13	14	15	16	17 Miles	18
19	20 Brittany	21	22 Franco	23 Miranda	24	25
26	27	28 Betsy	29	30	31 Claire	

1. Who is the helper in the second row of the fourth column? _____

2. Who is the helper in the fourth row of the second column?

_____

3. Who is the helper in the third row of the sixth column?

_____

4. Who is the helper in the fifth row of the third column?

_____

5. Who is the helper in the first row of the fifth column?

_____

Add or Subtract

Learn

Use Word Clues

How many in all? means add.
How many more? means subtract.

How many birds in all? $4 + 2 = 6$

How many more owls
than doves? $4 - 2 = 2$

What Can I Do?
How do I know whether to add or subtract?

Act It Out

Use counters. Act out the problem.

How many in all?
Think: I can put the
groups together
and count.

How many more?
Think: I can see
which group has
more and count to
find how many more.

Try It • **Look for clue words.
Write + or –. Then add or subtract.**

1.

How many more jays than owls?

5 ◯ 3 = _____

2.

How many in all?

6 ◯ 4 = _____

Name_____

Power Practice • Write + or −.
Then add or subtract.

3.

How many in all?

7 ◯ 2 = ____

4.

How many in all?

8 ◯ 5 = ____

5.

How many more doves than jays?

6 ◯ 4 = ____

6.

How many in all?

5 ◯ 5 = ____

7.

How many more owls than doves?

9 ◯ 4 = ____

8.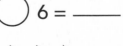

How many more jays than robins?

11 ◯ 6 = ____

9.

How many in all?

8 ◯ 3 = ____

10.

How many more jays than owls?

8 ◯ 7 = ____

More and Fewer

Learn

What Can I Do?
I want to know which group has more.

Use One-to-One Matching

Match. The group with items left over has more.

The group of spiders has more.

Count and Compare Numbers

Count and compare: 7 > 5.

The group of ladybugs has more.

Try It • **Match. Circle the group that has more.**

1.

Power Practice • **Circle the group that has more.**

2.

3.

Most and Fewest

What Can I Do?
I want to know which group has the fewest.

Count and Compare Numbers

Count the □s, △s, and ○s.

|1|2|3|4|5|6|7|8|

△1 △2 △3 △4 △5 △6

①②③④⑤⑥⑦

Write the numbers in order from the least to the greatest.

6 7 8

The group of □ has the most.

The group of △ has the fewest.

Try It • **Count and compare numbers.**

1. △1 △2 △3 △4
   |1|2|□|□|□|
   ①②○○○○

   The group of _____ has fewest.

2. △△△△△△△△△
   □□□□□□□
   ○○○○○○○○○

   The group of _____ has fewest.

Power Practice • Circle the group that has the fewest.

3.

4.

Subtract 2-Digit Numbers

Learn

Decide Whether to Regroup

$$\begin{array}{r} 66 \\ -44 \\ \hline \end{array} \qquad \begin{array}{r} 66 \\ -47 \\ \hline \end{array}$$

What Can I Do?
I want to subtract 2-digit numbers.

Think: I can subtract 4 ones from 6 ones without regrouping. I can't subtract 7 ones from 6 ones without regrouping.

No Regrouping   Regroup 1 ten 6 ones as 16 ones.

$$\begin{array}{r} 66 \\ -44 \\ \hline 22 \end{array} \qquad \begin{array}{r} {}^{5}{}^{16} \\ \cancel{66} \\ -47 \\ \hline 19 \end{array}$$

Add to Check

Check your subtraction by adding.

$$\begin{array}{r} 22 \\ +44 \\ \hline 66 \end{array} \qquad \begin{array}{r} 19 \\ +47 \\ \hline 66 \end{array}$$

Try It . Circle *Regroup* or *No Regrouping.* Then subtract.

1. $\begin{array}{r} 45 \\ -24 \\ \hline \end{array}$

2. $\begin{array}{r} 80 \\ -45 \\ \hline \end{array}$

3. $\begin{array}{r} 62 \\ -17 \\ \hline \end{array}$

Regroup

No Regrouping

Regroup

No Regrouping

Regroup

No Regrouping

Power Practice • Subtract.
Check by adding.

4. 22
  − 8

5. 83
  − 12

6. 76
  − 27

7. 43
  − 25

8. 94
  − 33

9. 67
  − 7

10. 32
  − 18

11. 65
  − 25

12. 46
  − 17

13. 94
  − 65

14. 54
  − 20

15. 58
  − 39

16. 23
  − 15

17. 67
  − 28

18. 55
  − 51

Mystery Bar Graph

Use the clues to fill in the bars on the bar graph.

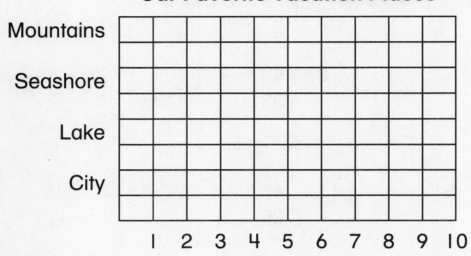

Our Favorite Vacation Places

Mountains

Seashore

Lake

City

1 2 3 4 5 6 7 8 9 10

Clues:

20 people were in the tally.

Each person chose one place.

4 more people chose Seashore than Mountains.

3 more people chose Mountains than Lake.

2 more people chose Lake than City.

I person chose City.

3-Way Data

Use this information.
Complete the tally, the bar graph, and the pictograph.

1. 4 people have dogs.

2. 6 people have cats.

3. 2 people have fish.

4. 1 person has a turtle.

5. 1 person has a snake.

Pets at Home	
Dog	
Cat	
Fish	
Turtle	
Snake	

Pets at Home

	1	2	3	4	5	6	7	8
Dog								
Cat								
Fish								
Turtle								
Snake								

Pets at Home	
Dog	
Cat	
Fish	
Turtle	
Snake	

Key: ☺ = 1 person

Explore Length

Learn

Line Things Up

Choose an object to measure.
Choose a tool to measure the object.
Line up the tool and the object at
the left side.

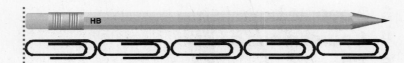

Think: How many clips long is the pencil?
I can line up the paper clips and
count them.

Count

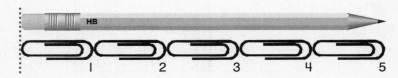
1   2   3   4   5

Think: The pencil is about 5 clips long.

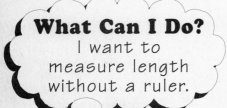

What Can I Do?
I want to
measure length
without a ruler.

Try It • **How long is each one?**

1.
1   2   3

_____ clips

2.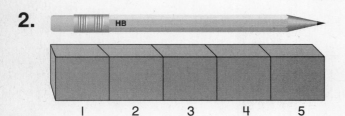
1   2   3   4   5

_____ cubes

Name_____

3.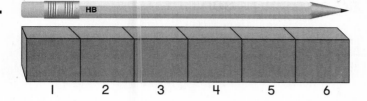

_____ clips

4.

_____ cubes

Power Practice • **How long is each one?**

5.

_____ clips

6.

_____ clips

7.

_____ clips

8.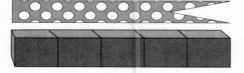

_____ cubes

9.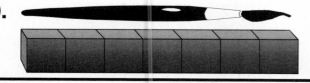

_____ cubes

10.

_____ cubes

Explore Capacity

Use Your Imagination

Look at the pictures.
Imagine using each one.

Think: When I take a bath, I use a lot of water. When I fill a glass, I use a little water. The bathtub holds more water than the glass.

Compare Other Measurements

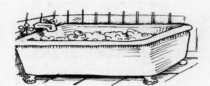

Think: The tub is longer than the glass. It is wider than the glass, too. It is also deeper than the glass. So, the tub must hold more than the glass.

What Can I Do?
I want to know which one holds more.

Try It • Circle the one that holds more.

1.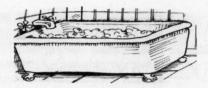

2.

Name_____

3.

4.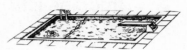

Power Practice • Circle the one that holds more.

5.

6.

7.

8.

9.

10.

Explore Weight

Learn

Use Your Imagination

Look at the object in each picture.
Imagine lifting each one.

Think: It is easy to lift a feather. A feather is light. It is harder to lift a bag of rice. A bag of rice is heavier than a feather.

What Can I Do?
I want to know which one is heavier.

Picture a Balance

Think: A feather would barely move the balance. A bag of rice would move its side down. A bag of rice is heavier than a feather.

Try It • Circle the one that is heavier.

1.

2.

3.

4.

Power Practice • **Circle the one that is heavier.**

5.

6.

7.

8.

9.

10.

Adding Three or More Numbers

Learn

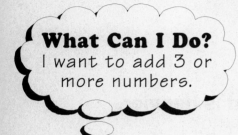

What Can I Do?
I want to add 3 or more numbers.

Look for 10

Look for numbers that add up to 10.   1
Add those numbers first.   3 ⎤
Then add the other numbers   4 ⎦
   + 7

Think: $3 + 7 = 10$, $1 + 4 = 5$, $10 + 5 = 15$.

Add in Stages

Add the first two numbers.   4 ⎤
Then add the third number.   2 ⎦
Then add the fourth number.   1
Check by adding the numbers   + 6
in a different direction.

Think: $4 + 2 = 6$, $6 + 1 = 7$, $7 + 6 = 13$.
$6 + 1 + 2 + 4 = 13$

Try It • Look for 10.
       Add.

1.   5
     4 ⎤
     6 ⎦
  + 2

2.   5
     2
     1 ⎤
  + 8 ⎦

3. $1 + 9 + 7 = $ _____

4. $5 + 4 + 5 + 4 = $ _____

Power Practice • Add.

5.
```
   6
   4
   3
 + 7
```

6.
```
   2
   2
   9
 + 8
```

7.
```
   5
   7
 + 5
```

8.
```
   4
   5
   1
 + 6
```

9.
```
   3
   7
 + 7
```

10.
```
   4
   4
   4
 + 8
```

11. $3 + 6 + 1 =$ _____

12. $4 + 7 + 3 =$ _____

13. $9 + 1 + 4 + 3 =$ _____

14. $5 + 5 + 6 + 2 =$ _____

15. $2 + 3 + 4 + 5 + 6 + 7 =$ _____

Compare Numbers

Learn

Use a Number Line

These numbers go up by one.
Numbers on the right are greater.
Numbers on the left are less.

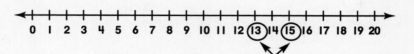

0 1 2 3 4 5 6 7 8 9 10 11 12 (13) 14 (15) 16 17 18 19 20

15 is greater than 13.   13 is less than 15.

Look at Place Value

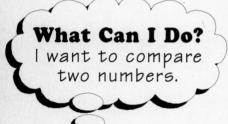

What Can I Do?
I want to compare
two numbers.

Compare the digits in the tens place.
Which digit is greater?

If both are the same, then compare the
digits in the ones place.
Which digit is greater?

tens	ones
1	3
1	5

Think: 5 ones are greater than 3 ones.
15 is greater than 13.

Try It • Use the number line.
Circle the number that is greater.

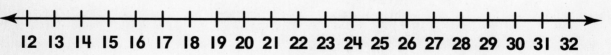

12 13 14 15 16 17 18 19 20 21 22 23 24 25 26 27 28 29 30 31 32

1. 12   21   **2.** 32   31

3. 30   29   **4.** 19   29

Name_____

5. 45   54   **6.** 33   23

7. 56   66   **8.** 69   70

9. 97   88   **10.** 17   16

11. 19   29   **12.** 80   79

13. 48   47   **14.** 47   57

15. 73   83   **16.** 82   28

17. 44   55   **18.** 50   5

19. 26   28   **20.** 59   58

Logical Length

Abner, Beth, Celia, and Danny have a frog-jumping contest. Use the clues and a ruler. Draw lines that show how far each frog jumped. Then answer the questions.

Clues

1. Abner's frog jumped 3 inches.

2. Beth's frog jumped 2 inches farther than Celia's frog.

3. Celia's frog jumped the same distance as Abner's frog.

4. Danny's frog jumped 1 inch farther than Abner's frog.

Abner's

Beth's

Celia's

Danny's

Questions

1. How far did each child's frog jump?

   Abner's: _____ inches   Beth's: _____ inches

   Celia's: _____ inches   Danny's: _____ inches

2. Which frog won? _____ 's frog

Five O'Clock Temperature

Read the weather reports.
Draw the line in the thermometer.
Show the temperature at 5:00.

February 24. The temperature at dawn was 5 degrees F. It went up 10 degrees by noon. By 5:00, it had dropped 5 degrees.

February 25. The temperature at dawn was 12 degrees F. It went up 8 degrees by noon and dropped 5 degrees by 5:00.

February 26. The temperature at dawn was 15 degrees F. It went up 15 degrees by noon and dropped 5 degrees by 5:00.

February 27. The temperature at dawn was 20 degrees F. It went up 12 degrees by noon and dropped 7 degrees by 5:00.

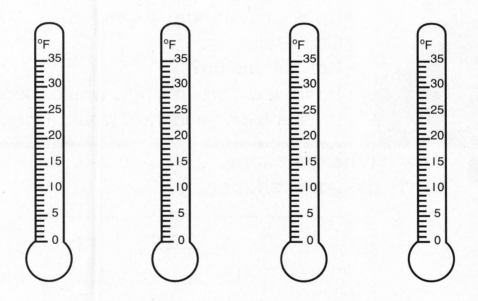

February 24   February 25   February 26   February 27

Same Shape

Learn

Look for Flat Faces

If the shapes are the same, the faces will be the same.

2 flat circles 6 flat squares 2 flat circles

What Can I Do?
I want to find which shapes are the same.

Ask Yourself Questions

Describe a shape by asking questions like these:

- Does it have a flat face?
- Does it have sharp edges?
- Can it roll?
- Can it stand up?
- If I turned it around, how would it look?
- If I stood it on end, how would it look?

Try It • Answer the questions.
Circle the same shapes.

1. Does it have flat faces? How many?				
2. Does it have corners?				
3. Can it roll?				

Name_____

Power Practice • Circle the same shapes.

4.

5.

6.

7.

8.

More About Same Shape

Learn

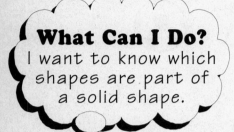

What Can I Do?
I want to know which shapes are part of a solid shape.

Trace a Solid Shape

If you traced around this solid shape, what shape would you see?

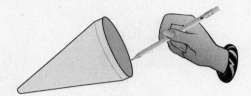

Ask Yourself Questions

Describe the faces of a solid shape by asking questions:

- Does the solid have flat faces?
- What do the faces look like?
- How many sides are there?
- Are the sides the same length?

Try It • **Find a block that looks like this. Trace around it. Circle the shape that you traced.**

1.

2.

Name_____

3.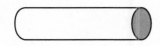

4.

5.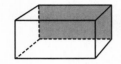

6.

7.

8.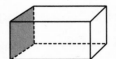

Sides and Corners

Learn

What Can I Do?
I want to know the number of sides and corners in a shape.

Trace and Count

Trace the sides. Count as you go.

A triangle has 3 sides.

Make Xs and Count

A corner is the place where two sides meet.
Make an X on each corner. Then count.

A triangle has 3 corners.

Try It
- Trace. Write the number of sides.
  Make Xs. Write the number of corners.

I.

_____ sides
_____ corners

2.

_____ sides
_____ corners

Power Practice
- Write the number of sides.
  Write the number of corners.

3.

_____ sides
_____ corners

4.

_____ sides
_____ corners

5.

_____ sides
_____ corners

Name_____

Equal Parts

Learn

What Can I Do?
I want to know if a line cuts a shape into equal parts.

Imagine Folding the Shape

If you folded the shape on the line, would the two parts match?

This line cuts the tree into equal parts.

Use a mirror

Place a small mirror on the line. Look at the shape. Do the parts match?

Try It • **Look at the fold line. Does it show equal parts? Circle Yes or No.**

I.

Yes   No

2.

Yes   No

Power Practice • **Circle the shape that shows equal parts.**

3.

4.

5.

Same Size and Shape

Learn

Imagine Lining Them Up

When you see two figures, imagine lining them up to face the same way.

Think:

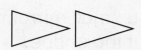

These are the same size and shape.

Trace the Figures

Use tracing paper.
Trace one figure.
Place it on the other figure.
See if they are the same.

What Can I Do?
I want to find if two figures are the same size and shape.

These are not the same size and shape.

Try It • Use tracing paper. Trace the shapes.
Circle the two that are the same size and shape.

1.

2.

Name_____

Power Practice • Circle the two that are the same size and shape.

3.

4.

5.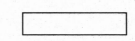

6.

7.

8. A ∀ A A

© McGraw-Hill School Division

Make New Shapes

Look at each shape.
Follow the directions.

Draw 1 line to make
2 smaller triangles.

Draw 1 line to make
2 rectangles.

Draw 1 line to make 2 triangles.

Draw 1 line to make 2 squares.

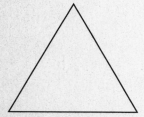

Draw 3 lines to make 1 square
and 3 smaller triangles.

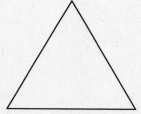

Draw 3 lines to make
4 smaller triangles.

Symmetrical Numerals

There are two ways to show that each of these numbers has equal parts.

If you fold these numbers along either line, the parts will match.

Write numbers that have matching parts. Draw lines to show the matching parts. You may use these grids to help you.

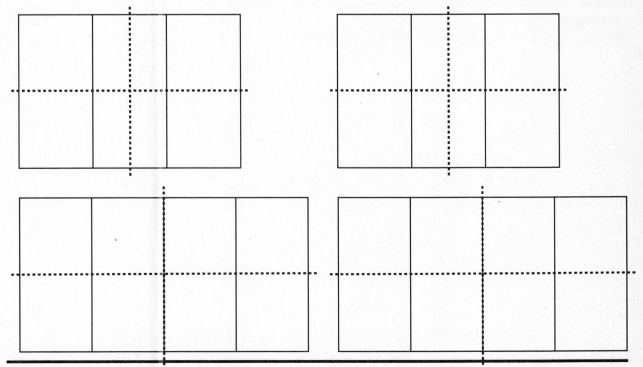

Equal Parts

Learn

What Can I Do?
I want to know the number of equal parts.

Number and Count

Find a place to begin.
Count.
Number the parts.

This circle has 4 equal parts.

Make Sure Parts Are Equal

This circle has 3 equal parts.

The parts are the same size and shape.

This circle has 3 parts that are not equal.

Try It • **Count. Write the number of equal parts.**

1.

_____ equal parts

2.

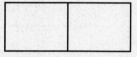

_____ equal parts

3.

_____ equal parts

4.

_____ equal parts

Name_____

Power Practice • Write the number of equal parts.

5.

_____ equal parts

6.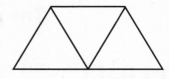

_____ equal parts

7.

_____ equal parts

8.

_____ equal parts

9.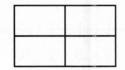

_____ equal parts

10.

_____ equal parts

11.

_____ equal parts

12.

_____ equal parts

13.

_____ equal parts

14.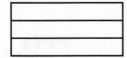

_____ equal parts

Greater Than and Less Than

Learn

Understand the Symbols

The symbol > means "greater than."
The open side of the symbol is next to the greater number.

$\qquad$ 5 > 3 means 5 is greater than 3.

The symbol < means "less than."
The symbol points to the smaller number.

$\qquad$ 3 < 5 means 3 is less than 5.

Use a Number Line

Greater numbers are always on the right.
Lesser numbers are always on the left.

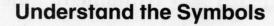

0 1 2 3 4 5 6 7 8 9 10

Think: 5 is to the right of 3, so 5 > 3.

What Can I Do?
I want to compare two numbers using >, <, or =.

Try It . **Use the number line. Compare.**
Write >, <, or =.

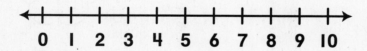

0 1 2 3 4 5 6 7 8 9 10

1. 6 ◯ 7 $\qquad$ **2.** 3 ◯ 3 $\qquad$ **3.** 8 ◯ 10

Power Practice • **Compare. Write >, <, or =.**

4. 12 ◯ 10 $\qquad\qquad$ **6.** 5 ◯ 5

5. 6 ◯ 16 $\qquad\qquad$ **7.** 15 ◯ 16

Name_____

Parts of a Group

Learn

What Can I Do?
I want to know how many objects are in one part of a group.

Find the Parts

This group has different parts.

2 buttons are large and white.
3 buttons are small and black.
1 button is fancy and gray.

There are 3 different kinds of buttons.
There are 3 parts of the group.

Count, Circle, Count

Count how many in all.
Circle the ones that belong together.
Count the objects in each circle.

Try It • Count, circle, and count. Write how many.

1. How many in all? _____   **2.** How many  ? _____

Power Practice • Write how many.

| Z | X | W | Z | Y | X | Z | Z | X | Z | Y | Z |

3. How many in all? _____   **4.** How many Xs? _____

5. How many Zs? _____   **6.** How many Ws? _____

Certain, Maybe, Impossible

Learn

Is It Possible?

Is it possible to pick a quarter?
Is it possible to pick a nickel?

Think: There are no quarters.
So, picking a quarter is impossible.
There are no nickels.
So, picking a nickel is impossible.

Decide Between Certain and Maybe

What Can I Do?
I want to know if something could happen or could not happen.

If you pick one coin, what could it be?

Think: All the coins are pennies.
So, picking a penny is certain.

If you pick one coin, what could it be?

Think: Some coins are pennies.
Picking a penny could happen.
Some coins are dimes.
Picking a dime could happen.
So, picking a penny and picking a dime are both "maybes."

Name_____

Try It . **Could it happen? Answer the questions.**
Circle the correct choice or choices.

1. Which pick is impossible?

2. Which picks are "maybes"?

3. Which picks are impossible?

4. Which pick is certain?

Power Practice . **Could it happen? Circle** *certain,*
maybe, **or** *impossible.*

5. 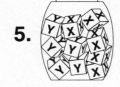 You pick a .   certain   maybe   impossible

6.  You pick a .   certain   maybe   impossible

7. 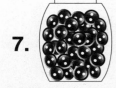 You pick a .   certain   maybe   impossible

Adding and Subtracting Fractions

Use red, blue, and green crayons.
Color the fractions.
Solve the problems.

Molly = Color it red.
Sally = Color it blue.
Billy = Color it green.

Molly ate $\frac{1}{8}$.

Sally ate $\frac{2}{8}$.

Billy ate $\frac{3}{8}$.

What fraction is left? _____

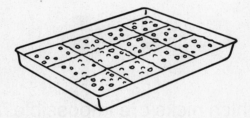

Molly ate $\frac{3}{12}$.

Sally ate $\frac{4}{12}$.

Billy ate $\frac{1}{12}$.

What fraction is left? _____

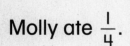

Molly ate $\frac{1}{4}$.

Sally ate $\frac{2}{4}$.

Billy ate $\frac{1}{4}$.

What fraction is left? _____

Name_____

Number Experiment

You will need a paper bag and six tagboard strips.
Write each of these numbers on a strip:

| 3 | 7 | 11 | 24 | 48 | 100 |

Put the strips in the bag.

Which kind of number will you pick most often?
Circle your guess.

one-digit number   two-digit number   three-digit number

1. Shake the bag.
2. Pick a number.
3. Make a tally mark on the chart.
4. Put the number back.

Do this 20 times in all. Was your guess correct?

Number	Tally
3	
7	
11	
24	
48	
100	

Numbers to 100

Learn

What Can I Do?
I want to write numbers to 100.

Skip Count by 10s

Count by tens.
Then count on by ones.

Think: 10, 20, 30; 31, 32, 33, 34.

Think About Place Value

Remember that tens
are on the left.
Ones are on the right.

2 tens, 3 ones = 23

Try It • **Skip count by tens. Then count on by ones.
Write how many.**

1.

10, _____; _____, _____, _____, 24, _____

2.
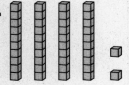

10, _____, _____, _____; _____, _____

Name_____

3.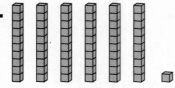

_____, _____, _____, _____, _____, _____; _____

4.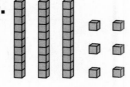

_____, _____, _____; _____, _____, _____, _____, _____, _____

5.

_____; _____, _____, _____, _____, _____, _____, _____, _____

Power Practice • **Write how many.**

6.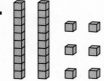

_____

7.

_____

8.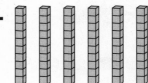

_____

9.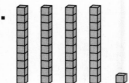

_____

10.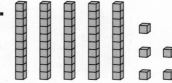

_____

11.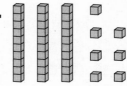

_____

Name_____

Tens and Ones

Learn

Skill Builder CHAPTER 12

Think About Place Value

Remember that tens are on the left.
Ones are on the right.

Think: 4 tens, 5 ones = 45

tens	ones
4	5

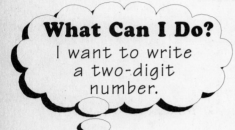

What Can I Do?
I want to write a two-digit number.

Circle Tens

Circle groups of ten.
Count the number left over.
Then write the number using tens and ones.

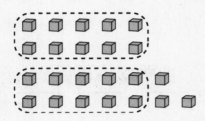

Think: 2 tens, 3 ones = 23

Try It • Circle tens. Write the number.

1. _____

2. _____

3. _____

4. _____

© McGraw-Hill School Division

Think: 2 tens, 3 ones = 23

104 Grade 2, Chapter 12, Cluster A

Power Practice • Write the number.

5.

tens	ones
4	6

_____

6.

tens	ones
7	2

_____

7.

tens	ones
8	3

_____

8.

tens	ones
3	5

_____

9.

tens	ones
5	1

_____

10.

tens	ones
1	7

_____

11.

tens	ones
2	9

_____

12.

tens	ones
6	7

_____

13.

tens	ones
9	8

_____

14.

tens	ones
2	4

_____

Number Patterns

Learn

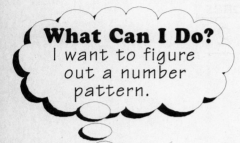

I want to figure out a number pattern.

Read this pattern:

36, 37, 38, 39, 40, ___?___

Think: 37 is 1 more than 36.
38 is 1 more than 37.
39 is 1 more than 38. The rule is Add One.

Read the Pattern Aloud

Reading aloud helps you "hear" the pattern.
Try reading these numbers aloud.
What number comes next?

44, 45, 46, 47, 48, ___?___
23, 33, 43, 53, 63, ___?___

Find the Rule

Read this pattern:

34, 44, 54, 64, 74, ___?___

Think: 44 is 10 more than 34.
54 is 10 more than 44.
64 is 10 more than 54. The rule is Add Ten.

Name_____

• **Find the rule.**
Circle it.

1. 11, 21, 31, 41, 51   Add One   Add Ten

2. 68, 69, 70, 71, 72   Add One   Add Ten

3. 97, 98, 99, 100, 101   Add One   Add Ten

4. 46, 56, 66, 76, 86   Add One   Add Ten

5. 19, 29, 39, 49, 59   Add One   Add Ten

Power Practice • **Write the missing numbers**
in each counting pattern.

6. 20, 30, _____, 50, 60, _____

7. 43, _____, 45, 46, 47, _____

8. 15, 25, _____, _____, 55, 65

9. 26, 27, _____, 29, _____, 31

10. 33, 43, _____, 63, 73, _____

11. 48, _____, 50, 51, 52, _____

12. 42, 52, _____, _____, 82, 92

Compare Numbers

Learn

What Can I Do?
I want to compare two numbers.

Use a Number Line

These numbers go up by ones.
Numbers on the right are greater.
Numbers on the left are less.

0 1 2 3 4 5 6 7 8 9 10 11 12 13 14 15 16 17 18 19 20

19 is greater than 9. So 19 > 9.
9 is less than 19. So 9 < 19.

Look at Place Value

Compare the digits in the tens place.
Which digit is greater?

If both digits are the same,
compare the digits in the ones place.
Which digit is greater?

tens	ones
3	5
3	4

Think: 5 ones is greater than 4 ones.
So, 35 is greater than 34.

Try It • **Use the place-value charts. Circle the number that is greater.**

1.
tens	ones
2	5
5	2

2.
tens	ones
3	1
3	2

3.
tens	ones
7	3
5	3

4.
tens	ones
8	7
8	8

Power Practice • **Compare. Write >, <, or =.**

5. 38 ◯ 83

6. 44 ◯ 43

7. 19 ◯ 91

8. 89 ◯ 90

9. 27 ◯ 25

10. 31 ◯ 30

11. 11 ◯ 11

12. 65 ◯ 55

13. 69 ◯ 70

14. 97 ◯ 97

15. 78 ◯ 79

16. 65 ◯ 56

17. 53 ◯ 33

18. 30 ◯ 3

19. 66 ◯ 68

20. 100 ◯ 10

Order Numbers

Learn

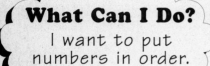

What Can I Do?
I want to put numbers in order.

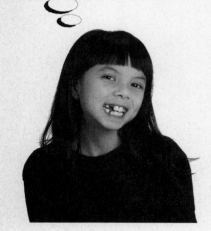

Use a Hundred Chart

The numbers are in order from least to greatest.

1	2	3	4	5	6	7	8	9	10
11	12	13	14	15	16	17	18	19	20
21	22	23	24	25	26	27	28	29	30
31	32	33	34	35	36	37	38	39	40
41	42	43	44	45	46	47	48	49	50
51	52	53	54	55	56	57	58	59	60
61	62	63	64	65	66	67	68	69	70
71	72	73	74	75	76	77	78	79	80
81	82	83	84	85	86	87	88	89	90
91	92	93	94	95	96	97	98	99	100

Think: 36 is just before 37.
38 is just after 37.
37 is between 36 and 38.

Count On or Back

Start with one number, such as 78.
Count on 1. One more is 79.
79 is just after 78.

Start with the same number, 78.
Count back 1. One less is 77.
77 is just before 78.
78 is between 77 and 79.

Name_____

Try It . Use the hundred chart. Write the number
that comes just before, just after, or between.

1. just after 44 _____

2. between 85 and 87 _____

3. just before 69 _____

4. just after 31 _____

5. between 49 and 51 _____

6. just before 27 _____

1	2	3	4	5	6	7	8	9	10
11	12	13	14	15	16	17	18	19	20
21	22	23	24	25	26	27	28	29	30
31	32	33	34	35	36	37	38	39	40
41	42	43	44	45	46	47	48	49	50
51	52	53	54	55	56	57	58	59	60
61	62	63	64	65	66	67	68	69	70
71	72	73	74	75	76	77	78	79	80
81	82	83	84	85	86	87	88	89	90
91	92	93	94	95	96	97	98	99	100

Power Practice . Write the number that comes
just before, just after, or between.

7. just after 17 _____   **8.** between 55 and 57 _____

9. just before 96 _____   **10.** just after 64 _____

11. between 76 and 78 _____   **12.** just before 21 _____

13. just after 8 _____   **14.** between 93 and 95 _____

15. just before 2 _____   **16.** just after 72 _____

17. between 81 and 83 _____   **18.** just before 100 _____

19. just after 19 _____   **20.** between 19 and 21 _____

21. just before 40 _____   **22.** just after 86 _____

Write the Numbers

**Answer the questions.
Then use the digits you write
to write as many different
3-digit numbers as you can.**

How old are you? _____

What is the first digit in your street address? _____

What is the last digit in your phone number? _____

Changing Patterns

Each of these patterns changes along the way.
Find the rule.
Draw a line where the pattern changes.
The first one is done for you.

1. 2, 4, 6, 8, 10, | 20, 30, 40

2. 5, 10, 15, 25, 35, 45, 55, 65

3. 10, 20, 30, 40, 50, 52, 54, 56

4. 2, 12, 22, 32, 42, 52, 62, 64

5. 8, 18, 28, 38, 48, 52, 56, 60

6. 100, 90, 80, 75, 70, 65, 60, 55

7. 41, 43, 45, 49, 53, 57, 61, 65

8. 35, 135, 235, 335, 435, 535, 735, 935

Add Tens

Learn

What Can I Do?
I want to add tens.

Use Addition Facts

Think: $3 + 4 = 7$,
so $30 + 40 = 70$.
$5 + 1 = 6$,
so $50 + 10 = 60$.

Draw a Picture

Picture tens blocks.
Add them.

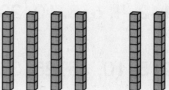

Think: $4 + 2 = 6$,
so 4 tens + 2 tens = 6 tens
6 tens = 60

Try It • Add.

1. $3 + 5 =$ _____, so $30 + 50 =$ _____.

2. $8 + 1 =$ _____, so $80 + 10 =$ _____.

3. $2 + 7 =$ _____, so $20 + 70 =$ _____.

4. $3 + 2 =$ _____, so $30 + 20 =$ _____.

Power Practice • Add.

5. $\begin{array}{r} 20 \\ + 40 \\ \hline \end{array}$ 6. $\begin{array}{r} 30 \\ + 10 \\ \hline \end{array}$ 7. $\begin{array}{r} 10 \\ + 70 \\ \hline \end{array}$ 8. $\begin{array}{r} 50 \\ + 40 \\ \hline \end{array}$ 9. $\begin{array}{r} 60 \\ + 20 \\ \hline \end{array}$ 10. $\begin{array}{r} 40 \\ + 40 \\ \hline \end{array}$

Addition Facts to 20

Learn

Use Doubles

Think about doubles.

2 + 2 = 4	6 + 6 = 12
3 + 3 = 6	7 + 7 = 14
4 + 4 = 8	8 + 8 = 16
5 + 5 = 10	9 + 9 = 18

Think: 5 + 6 is like 5 + 5 + 1.

5 + 6 = 11

8 + 7 is like 8 + 8 − 1.

8 + 7 = 15

What Can I Do?
I want to
add facts to 20.

Use Turnaround Facts

If you know one fact, then you really know two facts.

Think: 4 + 5 = 9, so 5 + 4 = 9.

8 + 6 = 14, so 6 + 8 = 14.

	tens	ones
		6
+		7
	1	3

Try It • **Add.**

1. 5 + 5 = _____, so 5 + 4 = _____.

2. 7 + 7 = _____, so 7 + 6 = _____.

3. 9 + 9 = _____, so 9 + 10 = _____.

4. 7 + 4 = _____, so 4 + 7 = _____.

Power Practice • **Add**

5.	6.	7.	8.	9.	10.
7	2	9	6	3	9
+ 8	+ 9	+ 4	+ 8	+ 7	+ 6

Add 2-Digit Numbers

Learn

Decide Whether to Regroup

$$\begin{array}{r} 26 \\ + 43 \\ \hline \end{array} \qquad \begin{array}{r} 26 \\ + 47 \\ \hline \end{array}$$

Think: I can add 6 ones and 3 ones without regrouping. I can't add 6 ones and 7 ones without regrouping.

No Regrouping	Regroup 13 ones as 1 ten 3 ones.

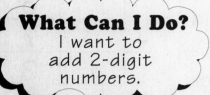

What Can I Do?
I want to add 2-digit numbers.

$$\begin{array}{r} 26 \\ + 43 \\ \hline 69 \end{array} \qquad \begin{array}{r} {}^{1} \\ 26 \\ + 47 \\ \hline 73 \end{array}$$

Add the Other Way to Check

Check addition by adding in the other direction.

$$\begin{array}{r} 43 \\ + 26 \\ \hline 69 \end{array} \qquad \begin{array}{r} {}^{1} \\ 47 \\ + 26 \\ \hline 73 \end{array}$$

Try It . Circle *Regroup* or *No Regrouping*.
Then add.

1. $\begin{array}{r} 55 \\ + 34 \\ \hline \end{array}$ Regroup   No Regrouping

2.   28
     + 17   Regroup   No Regrouping

3.   24
     + 48   Regroup   No Regrouping

Power Practice • **Add. Check by adding in the other direction.**

4.   32
     + 8

5.   40
     + 22

6.   57
     + 27

7.   33
     + 29

8.   64
     + 31

9.   65
     + 6

10.   42
      + 52

11.   35
      + 45

12.   86
      + 12

13.   14
      + 68

14.   21
      + 67

15.   47
      + 39

16.   13
      + 18

17.   53
      + 8

18.   46
      + 19

Round to the Nearest Hundred

Learn

Use a Number Line

The number 222 is between 200 and 300.
It is closer to 200.

So 222 rounds down to 200.

The number 275 is between 200 and 300.
It is closer to 300.

So 275 rounds up to 300.

What Can I Do?
I want to round a number to the nearest hundred.

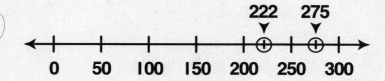

Use the Digit in the Tens Place

Look at the tens digit.
If it is less than 5, round down.
If it is 5 or greater, round up.

Round 149 down to 100.
Round 150 up to 200.

Try It . Use the number line.
Round to the nearest hundred.

1. 130 _____

    100 110 120 130 140 150 160 170 180 190 200

2. 580 _____

    500 510 520 530 540 550 560 570 580 590 600

3. 320 _____

    300 310 320 330 340 350 360 370 380 390 400

4. 258 _____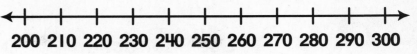

5. 441 _____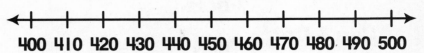

Power Practice • **Round each number to the nearest hundred.**

6. 730 _____   **7.** 195 _____

8. 253 _____   **9.** 543 _____

10. 236 _____   **11.** 858 _____

12. 142 _____   **13.** 659 _____

14. 75 _____   **15.** 360 _____

16. 715 _____   **17.** 907 _____

18. 455 _____   **19.** 346 _____

20. 188 _____   **21.** 220 _____

Subtract Tens

Learn

What Can I Do?
I want to subtract tens.

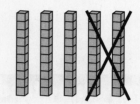

Use Subtraction Facts

Think: 9 − 4 = 5,
so 90 − 40 = 50.

6 − 3 = 3,
so 60 − 30 = 30.

Draw a Picture

Picture tens blocks.
Subtract them.

Think: 5 − 2 = 3,
so 5 tens − 2 tens =
3 tens.
3 tens = 30

Try It • Subtract.

1. 6 − 5 = _____,   so   60 − 50 = _____.

2. 7 − 2 = _____,   so   70 − 20 = _____.

3. 4 − 1 = _____,   so   40 − 10 = _____.

4. 8 − 4 = _____,   so   80 − 40 = _____.

Power Practice • Subtract.

5.	6.	7.	8.	9.	10.
40 − 30	30 − 10	60 − 40	50 − 30	70 − 40	90 − 50

Subtraction Facts to 20

Learn

Use Doubles

Think about doubles.

2 + 2 = 4	4 − 2 = 2
3 + 3 = 6	6 − 3 = 3
4 + 4 = 8	8 − 4 = 4
5 + 5 = 10	10 − 5 = 5
6 + 6 = 12	12 − 6 = 6
7 + 7 = 14	14 − 7 = 7
8 + 8 = 16	16 − 8 = 8
9 + 9 = 18	18 − 9 = 9

What Can I Do?
I want to subtract facts to 20.

Think: 13 − 6 is one more than 12 − 6.
13 − 6 = 7

Use Fact Families

If you know one fact, then you may know other facts.

Think: 15 − 8 = 7, so 15 − 7 = 8.
9 − 3 = 6, so 9 − 6 = 3.

tens	ones
1	6
	9

−

7

Try It • Subtract.

1. 14 − 7 = _____,   so   15 − 7 = _____.

2. 10 − 5 = _____,   so   11 − 5 = _____.

3. 6 − 3 = _____,   so   7 − 3 = _____.

Power Practice • Subtract.

4. 11 − 8 = _____   **5.** 14 − 9 = _____   **6.** 17 − 8 = _____

Subtract 2-Digit Numbers

Learn

Decide Whether to Regroup

$$\begin{array}{r} 55 \\ -\,33 \\ \hline \end{array} \qquad \begin{array}{r} 55 \\ -\,38 \\ \hline \end{array}$$

Think: I can subtract 3 ones from 5 ones without regrouping. I can't subtract 8 ones from 5 ones without regrouping.

No Regrouping   Regroup I ten 5 ones
                             as 15 ones.

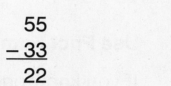

$$\begin{array}{r} 55 \\ -\,33 \\ \hline 22 \end{array} \qquad \begin{array}{r} {}^{4}\;{}^{15} \\ \cancel{5}\cancel{5} \\ -\,38 \\ \hline 17 \end{array}$$

Add to Check

Check your subtraction by adding.

$$\begin{array}{r} 22 \\ +\,33 \\ \hline 55 \end{array} \qquad \begin{array}{r} {}^{1}\;\; \\ 17 \\ +\,38 \\ \hline 55 \end{array}$$

> **What Can I Do?**
> I want to subtract 2-digit numbers.

Try It . Circle *Regroup* or *No Regrouping*. Then subtract.

1. $\begin{array}{r} 64 \\ -\,14 \\ \hline \end{array}$ Regroup   No Regrouping

2.   50
    − 25   Regroup   No Regrouping

3.   83
    − 14   Regroup   No Regrouping

Power Practice • **Subtract. Check by adding.**

4.   92
    − 6

5.   45
    − 32

6.   56
    − 17

7.   82
    − 48

8.   56
    − 21

9.   98
    − 57

10.   72
     − 58

11.   85
     − 29

12.   36
     − 18

13.   66
     − 65

14.   74
     − 26

15.   48
     − 29

16.   63
     − 35

17.   47
     − 28

18.   59
     − 21

Missing Numbers

Use place-value models if you need them.
Write the missing numbers.

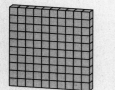

1.

hundreds	tens	ones
3	☐	5
+ ☐	4	6
7	1	☐

2.

hundreds	tens	ones
☐	2	5
+ 3	☐	5
5	1	☐

3.

hundreds	tens	ones
6	☐	2
+ 2	4	3
☐	0	☐

4.

hundreds	tens	ones
2	☐	5
+ ☐	6	7
6	0	☐

5.

hundreds	tens	ones
1	☐	9
+ ☐	4	5
3	2	☐

6.

hundreds	tens	ones
☐	9	7
+ 5	☐	4
7	4	☐

7.

hundreds	tens	ones
2	☐	8
+ 4	5	☐
☐	4	3

8.

hundreds	tens	ones
3	☐	8
+ ☐	4	5
9	3	☐

Missing Number Train

Use place-value models if you need them.
Write the missing numbers.

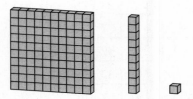

Hint: An arrow always points to the same number that it came from.

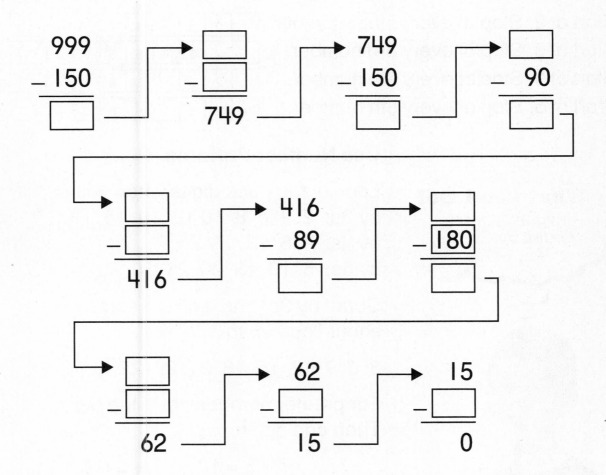

Skip Counting

Learn

Use a Hundred Chart

A hundred chart shows all the numbers from 1 to 100.

1	2	3	4	5	6	7	8	9	10
11	12	13	14	15	16	17	18	19	20
21	22	23	24	25	26	27	28	29	30
31	32	33	34	35	36	37	38	39	40
41	42	43	44	45	46	47	48	49	50
51	52	53	54	55	56	57	58	59	60
61	62	63	64	65	66	67	68	69	70
71	72	73	74	75	76	77	78	79	80
81	82	83	84	85	86	87	88	89	90
91	92	93	94	95	96	97	98	99	100

Start at 2. Stop at every other number.

Start at 3. Stop at every 3rd number.

Start at 4. Stop at every 4th number.

Start at 5. Stop at every 5th number.

1	2	3	4	5	6	7	8	9	10

1	2	3	4	5	6	7	8	9	10

1	2	3	4	5	6	7	8	9	10

1	2	3	4	5	6	7	8	9	10

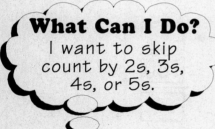

What Can I Do?
I want to skip count by 2s, 3s, 4s, or 5s.

Use Number Patterns

Look at the ones digits when you count

by 2s: 2 4 6 8 10 12 14 16 18 20

by 4s: 4 8 12 16 20 24 28 32 36 40

by 5s: 5 10 15 20 25 30 35 40 45 50

Count by 3s. The digits in each number should add up to 3, 6, or 9.

3 6 9 12 15 18 21 24 27

For greater numbers, add the digits. Then add again.

75   7 + 5 = 12   1 + 2 = 3

Name_____

Try It • **Fill in the missing numbers.**

1.

1	2	3	4	5	6	7	8	9	
11	12	13	14		16	17	18	19	20
21	22	23	24		26	27	28	29	
31	32	33	34		36	37	38	39	40

2.

71	72	73	74	75	76	77	78	79	80
	82	83		85	86		88	89	
91	92		94	95	96	97	98	99	100

Power Practice • **Write the missing numbers in each skip counting pattern.**

3. 60, _____, 70, 75, 80, _____

4. 21, 24, _____, _____, 33, 36

5. 64, 68, _____, 76, _____, 84

6. 40, 44, _____, 52, _____, 60

7. 30, 35, _____, _____, 50, 55

8. 86, 88, _____, _____, _____, 96

9. 54, 57, _____, _____, 66, 69

10. 62, _____, 66, 68, 70, _____

Equal Groups

Learn

Number and Count

First, number the groups.

Count. There are 4 groups.

Then count the number in each group. There are 3 in each group.

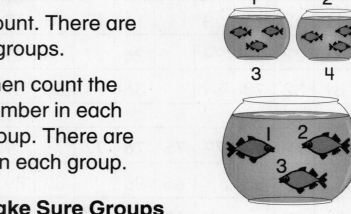

What Can I Do?
I want to know how many groups there are and how many are in each group.

Make Sure Groups Are Equal

In this picture, there are 3 equal groups.

This picture shows 3 groups that are not equal.

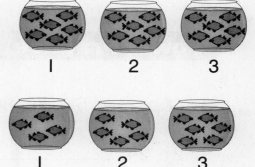

Try It • Number and Count. Write the number of groups. Write how many are in each group.

1.

2.

_____ groups

_____ in each group

_____ groups

_____ in each group

Name_____

Power Practice
• Write the number of groups.
  Write how many are in each group.

3.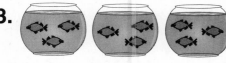

_____ groups of _____

4.

_____ groups of _____

5.

_____ groups of _____

6.

_____ groups of _____

7.

_____ groups of _____

8.

_____ groups of _____

9.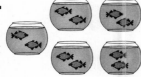

_____ groups of _____

10.

_____ groups of _____

Write a Number Sentence

Learn

Choose the Operation

Look at the picture. Decide whether to add or subtract. Choose + or − for your number sentence.

Think: The planes are all the same. One group is joining another. I can add to find how many in all. 7 + 6 = 13

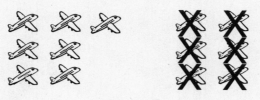

Think: There are 13 planes in all. 6 are crossed out. I can subtract to find out how many are left. 13 − 6 = 7

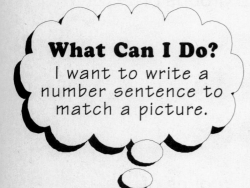

What Can I Do?

I want to write a number sentence to match a picture.

Use Numbers from the Picture

Think: I can count to find how many in all. One group has 6. One group has 7. 6 + 7 = 13

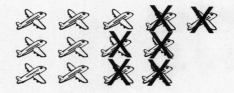

Think: I can count how many in all. I can count the number being subtracted. There are 13 in all. Six are being subtracted. 13 − 6 = 7

Name _____

1. ✈✈✗✗✗✗
✈✈✈✗✗
✈✈✈✗✗

___ ◯ ___ ◯ ___

2. ✈✈✈   ✈✈
✈✈✈   ✈✈
✈✈✈   ✈

___ ◯ ___ ◯ ___

Power Practice • Write a number sentence for each picture.

3. ✈✈✈✗✗✗
✈✈✈✗✗✗
✈✈✈✗✗✗

___ ◯ ___ ◯ ___

4. ✈✈   ✈✈✈
✈✈✈   ✈✈✈
✈✈   ✈✈

___ ◯ ___ ◯ ___

5. ✈✈   ✈✈✈
✈✈   ✈✈
✈   ✈✈

___ ◯ ___ ◯ ___

6. ✈✈✗✗✗
✈✈✗✗✗
✈✈✗✗✗

___ ◯ ___ ◯ ___

More About Equal Groups

Learn

Draw Lines and Count

Draw lines to show equal groups.
Count to check.
Make 2 equal groups.

Think: The line divides the stars into 2 groups.
There are 8 stars in each group.
The 2 groups are equal.

Make 2 equal
groups.

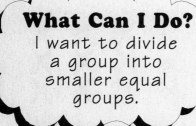

What Can I Do?
I want to divide a group into smaller equal groups.

Use Counters

Count out the same
number of counters.

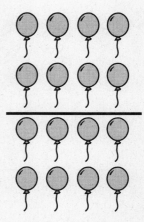

Place the counters in
2 equal groups.

Name_____

Try It • Use counters. Then draw lines to show the number of equal groups.

1.

Make 3 equal groups.

2.

Make 4 equal groups.

Power Practice • Draw lines to show the number of equal groups.

3.

Make 2 equal groups.
There are ____ in each group.

4.

Make 3 equal groups.
There are ____ in each group.

5.

Make 6 equal groups.
There are ____ in each group.

6.

Make 5 equal groups.
There are ____ in each group.

Find the Rule

**Use counters if you need them. Multiply.
Then write the rule.**

1. $0 \times 4 =$ _____ $3 \times 0 =$ _____ $0 \times 9 =$ _____

Rule: Any number multiplied by 0 equals _____.

2. $1 \times 3 =$ _____ $4 \times 1 =$ _____ $1 \times 5 =$ _____

$6 \times 1 =$ _____ $1 \times 7 =$ _____ $8 \times 1 =$ _____

Rule: Any number multiplied by 1 equals _____

_____

3.
$$\begin{array}{cc} 5 \\ \times 2 \end{array} \quad \begin{array}{cc} 2 \\ \times 5 \end{array} \qquad \begin{array}{cc} 3 \\ \times 4 \end{array} \quad \begin{array}{cc} 4 \\ \times 3 \end{array} \qquad \begin{array}{cc} 2 \\ \times 4 \end{array} \quad \begin{array}{cc} 4 \\ \times 2 \end{array}$$

$$\begin{array}{cc} 2 \\ \times 3 \end{array} \quad \begin{array}{cc} 3 \\ \times 2 \end{array} \qquad \begin{array}{cc} 8 \\ \times 1 \end{array} \quad \begin{array}{cc} 1 \\ \times 8 \end{array} \qquad \begin{array}{cc} 7 \\ \times 4 \end{array} \quad \begin{array}{cc} 4 \\ \times 7 \end{array}$$

Write a rule about the order in which you multiply two numbers.

_____

_____

Equal Groups in 48

Use 48 counters.
Find all the ways to make equal groups.

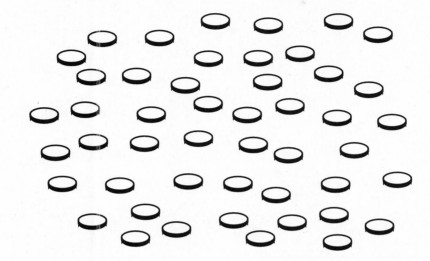

___2___ groups of _____

___3___ groups of _____

_____ groups of _____

_____ groups of _____

_____ groups of _____

_____ groups of _____

_____ groups of _____

_____ groups of _____

_____ groups of _____